TO
CATCH
A PASSING
UFO

TO CATCH A PASSING UFO

A Collection of Poetry
and Spoken Word

PJ

PHOENIX JAMES

TO CATCH A PASSING UFO

First Edition: 2024

ISBN: 978-1-7394810-9-4 (Paperback)
ISBN: 978-1-0685383-0-8 (Ebook)

Cover Artwork & Design by Phoenix James.
Book Design & Formatting by Phoenix James.

Visit the author's website at www.PhoenixJamesOfficial.com or email him at phoenix@PhoenixJamesOfficial.com

DEDICATION

To those who strive
To be better
To be greater
To those who know
There's more
Somewhere
Out there
Within
Without
From letting go
From holding on
They know
They will
Eventually
Find it
Be free from it
Or so they believe
In relinquishing
Thoughts
Fears
Doubts
Held onto
They let go
And arrive

And to a young boy
Now less afraid
To step away
And return
To home

I'm here
Over the moon
You didn't leave.

CONTENTS

ANDREI THE GREAT

Andrei the Great
How he got his name
Crowned by me
Coined by me
And given to him
Is how I met him
And what meeting him
And learning about his story
Signified for me
Where I had placed him
Based on the greatness
He had achieved
In a short space of time
Not only for himself
And his own life
But as a symbol
A great symbol for others
And in this story
Importantly, me
He had made this impression on me
That was great
So he was a symbol of greatness
That I aspired to
And he is the inspiration

I'd say
That sparked my decision
To finally get up and move
And do
And be disciplined
And change
And adopt
And adapt
And change old habits
And form new ones
And stick with them
And be better
He was the one where I'd say
Wow, that's inspirational
If he can do it, I can do it
This is a person
Not in a newspaper
Not in a magazine
Not on a television show
Not in a commercial
Not in a video
This is a real life person
You've seen do something
That you want to do
And it was just inspirational
And great

And his name was Andrei
And in my mind
He was Andrei the Great
Someone
Who had made those changes
For himself
And in doing so
Meeting him inspired me
And showed me
That if I made
The necessary changes
I too could achieve
What he had achieved
And that is the journey
I am on now
And inspired by
And continue to be inspired by
And I like to think
That my journey
Will inspire many others
Not only the story
Of Andrei the Great
But also the example he set
And the inspiration
He has given to me
By just being himself

And that rubbing off
And now me, living in that
Will rub off on others
Who encounter me and my journey
And how I'm living
And what I'm doing
It's important to say
That this was something
On my mind for a long time
You hear this, you see that
You know to yourself
I need to make these changes
I need to do this
I need to stop doing that
I need to stop eating this
I need to start eating that
I need to stop being lazy
I need to go to the gym
I need to exercise
I need to cut out this
Cut out that
And you go on like that
For a very long time
You can go on like that
For a very very long time
And that's what I was doing

And why I like to talk about
Who I call Andrei the Great
Is because meeting him in person
And hearing his story
And watching him
And seeing how he was living
And what he'd been through
In a very short space of time
That was the little thing
Just a little push over the edge
That was needed
For me to finally
Make my move
To do the same
And achieve the same for myself
It was already there
I had all the signs
I had all the inspiration
I had all the reasons
To go forth and be great too
But I hadn't met, in person
Another great
That was the little thing
The little change
The little tweak
The little push over the edge

The little last thing
That was going to make me get up
And do
And go for
And not look back
Meeting him that day
Was that moment
And thus
He shall be forever named
Andrei the Great.

ANYWHERE BUT HERE

A woman standing
By the side of a winding road
Flagging down a passing UFO
Stilettos
Tight jeans
And a bikini top
Tied at the neck
Hair pinned up
Bangles
Nails done
Suitcase
She's packed to go
Looking like she left home
In a hurry
To catch a passing UFO
I don't know
But I'd say
She figured it was time to go
Wherever a passing UFO
Might be heading
Some other galaxy out there
Somewhere far away from here
Some other place
In outer space

She looks nice
Dolled up and ready to go
Standing on the side
Of a winding road
Flagging down
A passing overhead UFO
Where she goes
Or hopes to go
No one knows
Somewhere
Better than here
I suppose.

ARE YOU OKAY

What happened
Where were you
When we were talking regularly
Where you are now
Is your life different
Are you a lot more settled now
Than you were then
Was a lot going on at that time
Were you just busy
With all the stuff
That you were talking about
Was it just work
Did you know
What was coming next
Is life always going
Where are you
In relation to that
Are you consumed
By what's pulling you
Or are you pulling it
Are you in control
Are you reading
Are you writing
Do you need a doctor

Do you have control
Are you more open
And willing
To allow things
Just to happen
And flow over you
Is this the best of life
Is it a huge readjustment
Have you ever lived like that
Have you always sort of tried
To not control
To let go of that
Are you a lot more
Spiritually awake now
Than you were before
Do you talk regularly
Do you remember
Where you were
When I was talking to you
About meeting others
Can you gauge it
From where you were
What was happening
Was it the first time
Do you remember
That conversation at all

Is it gone
Is it worrying
Or just normal
What can you recall
Were you trying to recall
Do you want to go back
And recreate that
Do you want to go back there
And have an understanding
Of where you were
Why does it matter
Where are you now
What do you want to do
Why is that necessary
To walk backwards
Where's that going to put you
If you do get there
Where's that going to place you
Where will you go from there
Will you come back here
What will you come back with
Why are you going back there
Can't you go forward where you are
Are you going back there to learn
To find what you haven't
Won't you be able to

Work it out as you go now
Were you in a different place
Spiritually
Than you were then
What benefit is it
What are you doing
Do you know
Is it energy
Can you go forward that much
It is because of what's happening
In your book
Does it tell you
Where you are
Can you go from there
Forward
And not back
Should we meet
Is that good
Did you see my message
Was it a positive lift for you
Did you need that focus
Is your head stuck
Do you feel stuck again
Is there a reason you're here
Are you getting some clarity
Do you need that opportunity

Is it great
Do you feel vulnerable
Did you say
You were vulnerable
Are you.

BIRTH OF THE FERAL PRINCESS

There's a saying
Much better to be
An old man's princess
Than a young man's slave
And maybe that works
Maybe it works for her
Maybe it works for him
Maybe it works for everybody
The longevity of a relationship
If she's married off young
It obviously worked back then
And was common practise
For a reason
One we've departed from
Somewhat
In this now modern
Independent
Liberated
And fast-paced
New world
Of equal rights and freedom
I imagine
If that's her first experience
Of being with a man

From young
And becoming his wife
Early in life
And doing
What married couples do
The things that
Preserve the relationship
Playing their roles
Male and female
Maybe it works out better
Long term
When she hasn't seen too much
Of the flashing lights
And shiny things
Maybe she's a bit more submissive
And less feral
And wild
And fine being that way
And less combative with him
And she's not feeling
Like her independence
Is being taken away
Like she's missing out
On something outside
Because that's all she knows
Is homely life

And they play
Their respective roles
He does his role
And she does her role
And that innocence
Hasn't been taken out of her
By the world
And her eyes are not opened
To all this other stuff
That seems better
Where it causes a breakdown
And deterioration
In the relationship
Because it's contrary
To what she's doing
And how she's living
When being
In that submissive role
Where she was protected
And provided for
And treated like a princess
It then seems
Like it's not that appealing anymore
When she looks outside
And she's been with other men
And she's done this

And done that
Maybe that is the better way
When she's younger
Starting out
And having that union early
I think
The way the world has gone
And where that idea started
The then and now
The two are not aligned
It's an old way
That doesn't fit the new world
But still is the right way
It's just a new modern world
That goes against
That old practice
Of women marrying young
The old way breaks that down
Into something that's not good
Or doesn't work
Or can't
It's very hard to make it work
In this new world
But in the old world
It was perfect
Or at least much closer to it

Before there was
All the distraction
Before there was this
New fast world
And people
Doing this
Doing that
Doing the complete
And total opposite to it
All of this, of course
Could be argued against
Disputed, opposed
At least in regard
To a time frame
Of where we all went wrong
If the story of Eve
The seductress
With the lustful spirit
And metaphorical apple
Is anything to go by.

COMPUTER DATING

I think
In this modern day and age
That the dating app
Serves its purpose
To connect people
Because everyone's busy
And everyone's face
Is in their screen anyway
So it's a good place
To meet people
And connect them together
Otherwise
They would have not met
Because maybe
One is in
This part of the country
And one
In another part of the country
Even another part of the world
Online dating
Is unlimited in that sense
But I think
What people tend to do
Is they connect online

But then they stay there
And they live there
Online
And they communicate there
For several weeks
Chatting, chatting, chatting
And never actually
Meeting each other
Some people are actually
More comfortable
With staying inside the app
They have no intention of meeting
Maybe they're just lonely
They like the attention
It feeds them
What they need at that time
They're not actually looking
To physically meet anybody
And that's fine
Everyone each to their own
There are others
Who feel safe there
They don't make any effort
To actually meet anyone
Because it's all
Right in the palm of their hand

So they're fine talking
Maybe some of them
Just lose track of time
And they're just
Texting, texting, texting
Building up this idea of a person
In their mind
And then
When they do
Eventually meet them
It's someone else
Because it's not the person
They thought it was
Or they've kind of
Misinterpreted them
You know
Made up this person
In their head
Based on information
They could read
Text characters on a screen
But couldn't see
The person's face saying it
Or hear the tone of their language
So they just
Assumed what they meant

And built up the type of person
They were talking to
Who is nothing like
The actual person
They're talking to
So I think it's
Counterproductive
In that way
I think once you connect
With someone that you see
And like the look of
You've read their bio
You've seen their pictures
And you have an interest
I think the next thing
Is to get off there
As soon as possible
And see if there is any kind of
Real viable connection
With them
In person.

CRAZY LOVE

I think
It's highly counterproductive
To stay on a dating app
Texting a stranger
Because there's nothing
Apart from
Words on the screen
To go by
Could you imagine
Texting someone for weeks
Then meeting
You had this
Whole idea of them
They had this
Whole idea of you
And none of it matched
Or translated in person
When you actually
Saw each other
That's the craziness
People are doing
In the hopes of meeting
Their ideal
Compatible person.

DAUGHTER OF THE SUN

During her visit to Africa
These two would meet

White mummy was nun
Black daddy was a priest

Both of them wanted some
So they went between the sheets

Between the hot Kenyan sun
And the sticky midnight heat

They had some freaky fun
Of which they couldn't speak

Became pregnant with a little one
She knew she couldn't keep

Would've been frowned upon
So she kept it all discreet

Placed her up for adoption
Little brown baby so sweet

She's a grown up woman now
With grown children of her own

It's mind blowing to think how
That was over fifty years ago

After people reluctantly came around
And the world wasn't so opposed

To mixed marriages being allowed
And interracial coupling wasn't a No

Things today differ somehow
I guess that's just the way it goes

She grew up in an all white family
The only brown girl of the bunch

Adoption isn't such a tragedy
When it comes down to the crunch

If she'd never had met her daddy
That would've been the punch

She reconnected with her birth mum
Who helped her find the priest

Overseas under the African sun
These long-lost two would meet

A Kenyan father and his daughter
Lay eyes for the very first time

Blood flows deeper than any water
That's what you say when blood cries

She now a grown mother, he a grandfather
Healing lives, making up for lost sunshine.

DESPITE THE WAR OUTSIDE

Fresh from the sun
And the war outside
She said it's been a long time
Since she saw me last
Said she needed to check
If that handsome guy
That she remembers
Was actually me
I said let me know
What you find out
She said, of course
But first I need to see you
The next thing we knew
We were alone together
Cosy, calm apartment
With a view
The perfect setting
For getting familiar
We were stuck to each other
Like glue
Embracing
Caressing and kissing
Like two young lovers after school
She said I'm sorry

And interrupted our play
I just started
On my period today
I didn't respond
I had nothing to say
Highly aroused
I carried on regardless
I didn't want to stop
What we'd started
Or to barter
Or to bargain
Or to think
I reached down
Into her underwear
And carefully found the string
Gently pulled out
Her soggy tampon
And threw it
Into the kitchen sink
I reached down once more
And slowly slid my fingers in
It felt warm
But dry from the tampon
But not at all dry for long
She quickly became wet
Wetter than wet

And then more wet
As I kissed her lips
And kissed her neck
And at the same time
Continued the caress
Slipping my fingers
In-between her legs
Inside her warm wet
Cavern of passion
Creating a smooth
Warm sticky mess
Turning my now soggy fingers
And the inside
Of her soft thighs red
Kissing me all over passionately
Moaning and breathing heavily
As her soft beautiful pussy bled
She looked at me with soft eyes
And told me I was crazy
As I lowered her panties
Down her thighs
Sliding my hard dick inside her
Slowly from behind
Spread across the kitchen counter
With a short sexy summer dress
Now way up above her waist

I pushed myself in deeper
As much as she could take
Groaning in bliss
And pure satisfaction
As we explored
More of this attraction
Despite the war
Raging on outside
We somehow
Found a place to hide
A safe place
A protective shelter
From the savagery
In action above
Shedding her own blood
As we passionately
Make love.

DON'T THINK ABOUT PAINTING

Perhaps you're concerned
About the time you've spent
Away from it
And it being perfect
When you do attempt it
Or opinions
Or worthiness
Or the size of a task, maybe
All can cause anxiety
Regrading starting up again
Some also call it
Imposter syndrome
Which often results
From extended breaks
Away from doing it
And then returning to it
I'm not sure
But what is for sure
Don't think about painting
Think about the feeling
You receive
When you're doing it
And how you feel
When you're satisfied

With what you've created
Ponder the works
You've enjoyed creating the most
Previously
And how satisfied
And empowered you've felt
And what you'd like to attempt
And create next
And sit down to paint
From that place
That perspective
Like a new fun experiment
Without pressure
For it to be perfection
An exercise
A play
A test
A clearing of the cobwebs
Painting is just like writing
When you feel that way
It's just a case
Of putting pen to paper
And finding your stride again
By the act of just doing
And doing again
Settling down

And picking up the brush
Is the hardest part
The rest just flows into itself
Once you just focus
On doing that
Just as it did before
When at your finest.

DURING THE COVID-19 CRISIS

The headline of my interview read
"Meet the new first aid volunteer
who selflessly threw himself into
supporting our logistics operation
after the pandemic hit."
I was asked
To talk about my role
I'm a Logistics Support volunteer
And during the COVID-19 crisis
I've been stationed
At East London Ambulance Hub
Where we are kept busy
Providing ambulance support
To the NHS
My role involves replenishing PPE
Items such as face masks
Gloves
Gowns
And face shields
Every day
So our ambulance crews
Will have the protection
They need
When responding to calls

I'm also responsible
For regularly recording
Medicine temperatures
Completing weekly
Hub stock report forms
Replenishing shelves
And cabinets
With equipment
And restocking our ambulances
In March
St John reoriented its whole operation
To support the pandemic fight
At the time
I'd just become a St John first aider
I completed my training
At the end of February
So I'd only just started
Attending Unit meetings
When the Coronavirus pandemic hit
Then once everything
Was in lockdown mode
I got an email
About volunteering
At the Ambulance Hub
And decided I would
I had no idea

What went on behind the scenes
During a crisis like this
Nor the important role
Played by logistics and equipment
In supporting the overall response
But it has been an amazing
And priceless experience so far
I have been so deeply involved
In a side of St John
I wouldn't otherwise have seen
I've been volunteering regularly
These past months
Both because I saw a real need
And because I enjoy helping others
It's good to know
I'm lightening the workload
Of the ambulance crews
Hub managers and other volunteers
On a typical shift
I'll sanitise door handles
And surfaces
Ensure radios
And LifePaks are charged
And set up everything
Necessary paperwork
PPE

Airwave radios etc
For the ambulance crews
Then I'll replenish PPE packs
Check stock levels
Request fresh supplies
Take deliveries
Log patient report forms
Scan ambulance crew
Deployment run sheets
Make phone calls
Jet-wash ambulances
And make sure the Hub is clean
And orderly
Some days, if time permits
I'll also cook breakfast
Or lunch for everyone
Then store some away
For the late-shift crews
Or refrigerate for another day
Basically, I'm there to help the crews
And hub manager any way I can
So I do whatever needs to be done
On that day or week
When I arrive home
My family is usually
Tending to the garden

Cooking up a new recipe
Or doing something creative
We'll often sit and eat together
Before the television
And chat
About the events of the day
Other than that
All this volunteering
Means that my washing is piling up
But as things slow down
I'm looking forward
To enjoying a lie-in or two
One thing should everyone know
About Logistics Support volunteering
It's a very varied role, for starters
Which COVID-19
Has made considerably more varied
The set hours of a shift
Aren't necessarily
The hours you will do
Since on some days
There is simply a lot more happening
Than the day before
And more things
Needing your attention
I've come to learn

That Logistics Support
Is a bit of an unsung
And unseen hero
Our importance at the hub
Lies in making sure
That St John ambulances and crews
Always have the correct equipment
Kit and resources
And in the right quantities they need
To go out there and save lives
Three words
That best describe my role
Since the pandemic hit
Are Key, Support, Volunteer
What has been a core difficulty
During the pandemic response
Has just been the difficulty
Of living within the constraints
Of the lockdown
With social distancing rules
Shielding
And self-isolating
And the psychological affects
And strain they can cause
At our virtual Unit meetings
People openly express

Their frustration
Of not being able to attend
Face-to-face Unit evenings
Nor participate
In our other normal activities
That's been a challenge for many
Myself included
But thankfully
St John
Is putting initiatives in place
To create activities
So our volunteers
Can still utilise their skills
And knowledge
While offering meaningful help
And support
The single aspect
About this whole experience
That gives me the most hope
For St John's future
At a time of such major uncertainty
Is that it has been inspiring
To witness everyone's ability
To come together
And work so well
Alongside each other

Seeing our people's resilience
And passion for problem-solving
Getting things done
And helping others
Is so educational
And rewarding
At this stage
I am looking forward
To growing within the organisation
And learning more
As I increase my knowledge
And skill levels
And I've especially
Enjoyed helping
Our newer logistics volunteers
During their first shifts
And walking them through
Everything that I've learned so far
After a busy day
Volunteering at the Hub
Not much can keep me awake
Once it's time to sleep
And recharge
Although
On non-volunteering nights
I can often stay up quite late

Watching my favourite TV shows
Or a good psychological thriller
One of the first things I'll do
Once we're given a full
Social all-clear
Is go along
To a regular Unit meeting
And hug
All my new St John family
And friends
I'll also attend
My first ever public event
As a first aider
Or logistics support volunteer
Or maybe both
And perhaps
I'll even explore volunteering
In other areas of the organisation
Whatever happens
It'll be yet another educational
Empowering
And amazing experience
With St John.

EYE CANDY OVERLOAD

Here she comes
Eye candy overload
You know you look good
And it shows
And if I could
I certainly would
Just so you know
I wouldn't say no
You look just right for me
Even though you just might be
Too much sweetness for me
But don't keep it from me
Just you keep it for me
How about you feed it to me
I'll surely eat it up all the same
All you have to do is say
And feel no need to explain
Anyway, what's your name
I want to get to know you
You and all that sugarcane
You and all of that honey
Dripping and sticking to me
Hot, melting and runny
I'm now just stuck on you
And you just walk by me
Smiling, like it's funny.

FEELING AGAIN

She said
She was thinking of me
That she missed
Those peaceful hugs
And forehead kisses
She missed me
Mr Poet
My company
My smile
My touch
My voice
My soulful eyes
That I'm simply amazing
Charismatic
Kind
A man that women dream of
She hoped it was okay
To express herself
And hoped to see me soon
This man
Who appreciates
Is very close to her heart
That I made her feel
A worthy woman

With my words
Actions
That every minute she was here
She felt she was special
That I showed her
What she was missing
All of these years being a woman
That she can't thank me enough
For every minute
I allowed her to be with me
Giving her a chance to know me
The pure soul that I am
That everything felt so calm
Peaceful
And good around me
That she has never been
So comfortable
Being naked
That my warmth
Hugs
Kisses
And every touch
Was communicating
With her inner body and soul
That she'd heard
Unfavourable comments

About her body
And that comparisons
To perfections
Has made her
Lose confidence in herself
She'd mentioned previously
That she was not feeling herself
That she's played two roles
All her life
Masculine as father
And feminine as mother
For her son
That she didn't have any option
When he left her
With a one year old baby
And never turned up
That she hasn't seen him
Since 2002
So in playing these roles
She many times forgot
That she's actually a woman
As fragile
And feminine
As everyone else
She too
Wished to feel like one

46

But there was no one
To ask her
Or treat her like one
Simple things
Like coming home
After long day
Putting her guard down
Feeling safe and sound
Knowing she is in loving
Safe hands
And being able
To sleep in peace
Has become a lifetime dream
That I gave her
That kind of boost
And hope
With my kind nature
That I filled her with affection
She was craving for
I gave her hope
It's still possible
I brought positive change in her
That she has read my books
And about my type of woman
That I shouldn't worry
That she is clear of my thoughts

With all respects
She believes
Everything happens
For a reason
That she was a little disappointed
With herself
Though I was giving her so much
That I have no idea
She wanted to give me
All she has
She felt like maybe
She wasn't able to turn me on
Or make me feel
That if so, it's a shame on her
That she's an over-thinker
And it's been on her mind
That she really wishes
To give me all of her
And make me feel
To my soul
As I made her feel
That she hopes
She won't be
A disappointment again
And that every word she said
She genuinely meant.

FOR MONKEY BRAINS

I called her this evening
Thought I'd add a voice to the face
She answered
Sounding pleased to hear me
Warm
Polite
Receptive
She apologised
For being out
At the shop with her boys
That she wasn't expecting me
Which I knew, so I didn't mind
I told her
I thought I'd give her a call
On this warm evening
She asked me about the weather
And where I currently was
I told her we'd been blessed
With a nice hot period
She apologised again
For being interrupted by her boys
While talking to me
I said, it's fine
I know you weren't expecting me

She said, sometimes that's more fun
She asked what I'd been doing today
Told her I was writing my next book
Said she'll have to check out my writing
And that it must be great
Said I was enjoying the journey so far
Said it's what she always wanted to do
When she was younger
To write
But never did
She became a special effects
Make up artist
For movies
So I said, she just started writing
On people's faces
She laughed
We laughed
We agreed it's all art
I told her I started out drawing
And then it all just turned into words
I said, I enjoy it
That it keeps me out of trouble
She said, I bet
And that maybe
She should start drawing
To which I said

Why, have you been getting into trouble
She said, No
But I miss those days though
I asked her, if the trouble or the drawing
She said, the trouble
I asked if those days were a distant memory
She said, Yes, but not too distant
That her friends are always reminiscing
We talked about being in our twenties
She said they were good days
I said, yes they were
And that I wish I could go back to them
And do a few things differently
She said yes, but
If you'd done them too differently
Would you be where you are now
I said that's the thing
No, I wouldn't be
She said, I guess it depends on
How you feel about where you are now
I said, that's a very true statement
Because anything you change
Would obviously
Put you in different position
She said, only just one
Tiny little different turning

And so much would be different
Big time, I said
She said, but you'll never know
If it's for the better or not
I said, to be honest
I quite like where I am
She said, well then
You wouldn't change too much then
I said, it would probably alter everything
If I changed one tiny little thing
I said, just think if you could go back
With the knowledge you have now
She said, wouldn't we all
That she'd be a millionaire
If she could go back
With the knowledge she has now
I said, oh we all would
Maybe a billionaire
I asked her about her boys
Two twins aged seven
And one thirteen, and one fourteen
We spoke about where we lived
How long we've been living there
And about how quickly
That time has passed
She asked if I liked where I live

To which I said yes
Something new, something different
Exploring a new space
I told her I spend a lot of time
With my head in my books
So when I come outside
It's always new
She said, yeah
You could be anywhere I suppose
I said, exactly, and it's always new
There's always things new happening
That I didn't realise were happening
Because I'm so busy working
I told her I thought it was amazing
That she was raising four little boys
She said, they keep you busy
That's for sure
I told her I know it's all photoshop
On her profile photos
But that she looked good
She laughed
She said, not all
And it's very, very slight as well
We laughed
She said, there is a few there
Especially ones that people post of me

Which actually I hate
When someone tags me in a photo
Because I haven't had control of it
And I swear
They pick the worst ones of you
To which I replied
They're probably saying
Who does she think she is
Always looking good all the time
I am going to post this one
The worst one of her
Nope, on second thoughts
That one is too good
I am going to post this one
We laughed
I then said, I had no Idea
That you were in my online network
I had no idea
I don't know how you got there
I don't know how you pulled that off
She said, she must have snuck in
She then said, I'll be honest with you
That it was months of planning
Months and months of strategic work
That eventually she worked her way in
I said, yes it would have to have been

That there's absolutely no other way
She said it took an awful lot
To break down the defences
But she made it
Well done, I said
It's never been done
She said, I'm glad you recognise my effort
I said, it would have to have been
A major effort, so I commend you
I said, I had come across
Her profile one day
That she must have posted something
And I said to myself, Okay, who's this
That I'd read what she posted
Though I don't remember what it was
And that I then saw her name
And profile photo, and clicked on it
Out of curiosity
And that's when I looked more
Into her work and what she did
Piqued your interest, she said
I said, Yes
She said she did prosthetics mainly
And special effects
But can't do it as much as she'd like to
As she can't do fourteen hour shifts

Said she gets the odd filming jobs
That her mother would take over
With the children
But that she can't do it often
With four kids
She said, so additionally
She also does filler and botox
As a sideline
She asked about me
Whether it was just writing I do
Or if had any sidelines too
I told her I have a few
But that they were all
Just branches of my writing
Into music, and film, and video
And theatre
She said, it's good to be creative
I said, yes it is
She said, it sounds busy where you are
I said, yes I've just stopped off
For a bite to eat
Because today
I can't be bothered to cook
Fair enough, she said
What are you eating
Chicken, I told her

Getting the protein in
We spoke a while
About children growing up
And sibling relationships
Disagreements and fights
How kids behave
And how we were as kids
She claims she was the good child
I asked her
What she was now doing
And where she now was
Said she was now sitting outside
I asked her if it was nice outside still
Because it looked
Like it had turned breezy
She said, it looks like rain
And that she's not going to go in
With everyone inside
While she's on the phone
Because of all the questions
She said, it would be who's that
Who are you talking to
That she's not allowed a life
I asked her, what is life
Outside of four children
And special effects etc

She said, work
And a lot of serious studying
That she's always learning something
I said that's my top thing, learning
Said she loves it
That she'd just done a counselling course
And that now she was doing an NLP one
That she loves psychology
I said, no way, tell me about that
She said it's amazing
You learn so many things
She said it's quite a new technique
That they only brought it out
In the seventies
A lecturer and one of his students
Took all of the knowledge on the subject
And put it into a new kind of system
Along with elements of hypnosis
She talked about triggering
And anchoring
And that it wasn't about manipulation
I said, I agree
I'd say it's about understanding
How the human brain works
And how to make use of it
In a positive way

She said, exactly
But when I try to explain it
It comes across like manipulation
But it isn't, she said
She said, sometimes you've got to
Take control of situations
And that really helps you
To do it in a positive way
I said, can I tell you something
She said, go on
I said, I went to someone's house
And heard my first example
Of what NLP was
When I was seventeen
I asked the person
To let me borrow the cassette
They gave me some tapes
And I've never looked back
I still have those tapes today
She said, I love it
I'm so interested in it
That I'm doing a course in it
And that she will be a practitioner
By the end of it
I said, that's amazing
She said it really is

That even if
She isn't doing one of the essays
Or the assignments
That's she'll flick through
All the paperwork
On things like
Where your eyes are looking
Whether you're looking from memory
Or if you're making something up
She said, it's so in depth, I love it
I said, it's good to talk to someone
Who is studying it
Because it refreshes
Certain things in my mind
Mirroring
And status changing
It just flashes it all back
She said, it's just trying to remember
To use it in everyday life
I said, it becomes habit after a while
She said she also finds
Especially in motherhood, for instance
If she's had a bad moment
She'll think afterwards
I know what I should have done then
I know how I could've done that

But that it goes out of your head
For a little while, during that moment
And you revert back
To your monkey brain
It's trying not to let
That side of your brain
Take over
That it's frustrating
When you know you've got these thoughts
But you forget to use them
We spoke about different NLP teachers
Popular names in the field
And how the first one you're exposed to
Tends to leave an impression
Something like a soft spot for a first love
Said she loves reading a proper book
That she has a Kindle
And that her mother keeps telling her
To download books onto her phone
But she likes holding an actual book
She likes the pages
I told her I love that
That she's a dying breed
Said she'll specifically wear a watch
Because she doesn't want
To use her phone for everything

I said I can totally relate
That we are losing a lot
With the use of smart phones
The humanity is going out of us
She said, teenagers today
Struggle with an analog clock
And that it's a shame
That it's dying out
How it's all digital now for the youth
She said, if I say it's quarter to
They say, what does that mean
We talked about age
And getting older
And remembering things
She said, the other day
She had a delivery driver turn up
Who asked for her date of birth
To which she replied, 1982
1992, he asked
She said, bless you, No, 82
She laughed
Said she thought he was probably
Either deaf
Or just being polite
I said, looking back now
Which do you think it actually was

She said
I think he probably didn't even look up
From the phone
Just thought he heard 92
We laughed
She said, she'd love to stay and chat
But that she had to go in
And get the kids to bed
But that I should definitely stay in touch
And to make sure I do
Because it's been refreshing
She said, stay in touch please
I said, okay
Well, you've got my number as well
If you've got a window
And you're thinking
That you'd like to speak to me
Just give me a shout
She said, I'll do that
I said, if I'm not at the other end
I will be, and I'll call you back
We told each other to take care
And each said, bye
And ended the call.

FREE HORSES

I am pleased to hear
That you're not waiting
For me anymore
It actually comes
As somewhat of a relief
To have you no longer
Wait around for me
It was to be expected
You're a woman with needs
And need someone
To have sex with
Though you only told me
Because I suggested it
That we be upfront and honest
If there's someone else
We're messing with
You say you still
Want to see me too
As I do the things
That he doesn't do
Which makes you feel
Like less of a whore
Since he just fucks good
And gives nothing more

I know you enjoy our talks
But from this day forth
Our movie is over
And my lips
Will no longer kiss yours
Or my hands caress your hair
Or touch you anywhere
Remember our last time
For that will indeed be the last time
Today I set you free
To wait no more for me
To stare deeply into your eyes
In the way you've been longing for
That next Friday
Will never come
For yourself and I
To be alone together
And spend the night
We shall no longer
Intimately intertwine
But never mind
It sounds to me
Like you'll be just fine
I'll reserve my bed
For someone else
Dear Sam can have you

To himself
I'll meanwhile
Save myself for selfishness
As sex with someone
We know we shouldn't
Is the wrong form of selflessness
Thus you will see
All of our imperfections
Closely
From a great new distance
Watch yourself
Carefully
It's often very hard
To tell an angel
And the devil apart
We go up
We go down
Wild and beautiful we remain
Nevertheless
Like free horses
Take another snapshot
Delete another flaw
Some things
We can't un-see or erase
They burn forevermore
Look into the mirror and see

You're everything
That you don't want to be
All the while still pointing
Your finger at me
Whinging and whining
Twisting and twining
We made love in our dreams
Like children playing make-believe
Our extended phone conversations
You say are better than sex
But yet
They will never be good enough
To satisfy your flesh
Love at first sight is a fantasy
An illustrious illusion
Sweet like honey to the mind
But bitter to the eyes
I'm glad you're not waiting for me
Women who have waited for me
Have mostly been disappointed
To find
We had no appointment appointed
I can't heal
Your hurting wounded soul
Anymore than Sam can
I'm sure you know this though

What your soul needs to heal
Isn't plans with man
But something much more than
Sex is only a temporary bandaid
For deep unhealed wounds
A fleeting and temporary measure
Like striking a match
To light a dark cellar
To find ones way
You expressed
You can be yourself with me
There's no need to pretend
You can ask me anything
You can tell me anything
Without being scared
That it might push me away
But some things shouldn't be said
Some things shouldn't be shared
Tell Sam
To want you for more than sex
Tell Sam to listen to you
And bring you hope
Tell Sam to help you heal
Tell Sam to look into your eyes
And speak to your soul
As no-one will ask

How you are today
As no-one will check on you
As you lay in bed
All alone with your thoughts
I can't look into your eyes
The same anymore
It is said the poet
Must not avert his eyes
But some things
I wish you didn't show me
I preferred the blindness
Absence creates
The naivety
The not knowing
The not seeing
The happy illusion
That the woman I'm being given
Is untouched
Untainted
Never before held
Unused
Clean
New
Unsoiled
No man wants to know
What the last man did

Or how good he did it
Or what he wants
To do to you
On a regular basis
Save the screen shots
Of your conversations
For your girlfriends only
Show them instead
The many ways
He wishes to slut you
Let another man
Live in his illusion
That there is some purity
Left in you
That your pussy
Is only for him
I don't need to know
How open-minded he is
That during sex anything goes
That he's down for anything
That accidents are okay
That getting things dirty is okay
That if you feel like squirting
You should let it out
That he doesn't mind at all
The nastier the better

And that you're seeing him
Tomorrow
And that it's what you like
With him
And that you were talking
About anal
And that you think it's not dirty
And that his name is Sam
You're right
He does deserve to have a name
He deserves to be mentioned
To be significant
To have a place
To be relevant
The be remembered
To be kept in mind
Between you and I
Whenever we lock eyes
And kiss thighs
And tell our lies
You said the best orgasms
In your life
Were during anal
With your lover who died
Well how does Sam
Measure up for size

Since you can't stop talking
Enough to hear
The uncomfortable moments
That you'd never understand
But so easily create
Keep on talking, talk away
This is great
Tell me how his balls
And his penis taste
Or how if felt
When he came on your face
In your mouth
And you swallowed it down
In fact, while I have this in mind
Kiss me now
So I can feel like
A part of the experience somehow
Nice and dirty
How you say you like it
And tell Sam what you told me
That you can't talk with him
Like you can with me
That you don't wait
For time with him at all
Like you do with me
That it doesn't matter

How good the sex is
That you'd rather talk to me by far
The hopeless romantic
Porn star that you are
Please stay yourself over Sam's way
In Sam's bed
We'll be making no plans today
That horse is dead
Flogged to death, with talk of sex
So pause, don't waste your breath
Save your texts, for Sam instead
And whoever's next
Wanting to hear
How you went somewhere
Had good sex and left
How it's so good
But when you leave
You forget
Needless to say
That I'm unimpressed
You'll have to share my piece
With some other silly guy
Dying to release
And empty his willy
Deep in your insides
This is where I get off

And leave him
To enjoy the ride
In this case
Your aptly self-titled 'shitty life'
This is a poem
You can call your own
As requested
I hope you like
Not quite a romantic love poem
But it will have to suffice
For what in this life
Are lovers
Who don't wish
Or know how to
Truly love one another
It should feel like heaven
Knowing you'll miss me like hell
And I know you will
You even said so yourself
But it's still
Somewhat bittersweet
To stop
And bid our little thing farewell.

IN TIME

Unfortunately, you're a poet
This is the tragedy
They'll say you're a freak
They won't approve
Of you seeking
To forge yourself a reputation
In the world of literature
They'll seek to burn your desire
Your fiery passion
Douse it like water to a flame
But you must rage
And burn bigger and stronger
And greater
Because you have to
They will learn
And you will find
Your proper place
Your immortality is at stake
In the end
When all the words are said
And all the deeds are done
The only name
They'll have ruined
Is their own

And those that follow them
They won't prevent you
From rising
Among them
Yours is the only name
That shall be remembered
And recalled
Discussed
Revered
Quoted
Mentioned
Studied
Many years from now
All will know your name
Your greatest moments
Captured on a page
From the words you've written
That the world will never forget
You have a purpose on this earth
To be a great writer
You never know
When your moment will come
But you can sense it coming
Just write
Let go
Lose control

Keep your mind on fire
A fire that cannot be put out
Keep writing
Your brain exploding with ideas
Let them ignite your soul
And with that, you write
Become the poem
Write hundreds
And thousands of poems
Right where you are
And wherever you go
Never stop writing
They cannot stop you
Write and write and write
Poem after poem after poem
And keep on going
Don't ever stop
It's important
It matters
Who cares
What they say
Who cares
What they think
They don't know you
They never did
But they will

And all those who come after
You don't need them
To acknowledge you now
Your voice will be heard
Forever
And for them
It doesn't even register
Yet
In time
Those who live long enough
Will all understand
That your poems are powerful
Too powerful
In time
You won't believe the reactions
To your writing
The reverence
The respect
Way above and beyond
The ridicule
And remarks
So write
Make your mark
Write whatever you want to write
Say whatever you want to say
Make whatever you want to make

Your poems
Are works of genius
Works of art
They need to be heard
They need to be seen
And they will
By all people
Get ready
Write
Be ready
To see
And be seen
And to witness
For yourself
The greatness of your creations
Your poems, your words
You won't remain invisible
The world will read your words
Everyone will see you
Everyone will hear you
All will feel you
Become who you already are
The world will know your name
You are not a nobody
Think your words
Speak your words

Write your words
Publish your words
Do not let them die inside you
Die with you
Write
Don't disappear from this earth
Without a word
Write
Write the love
Write the joy
Write the hurt
Write the pain
Just write the words
Just get to work
And let them remember your name
Don't worry, they will find you
You will not be hidden
You'll be famous
A famous poet
World famous
Perhaps even famous overnight
You're famous now
You just don't realise it
Just how much
You're discussed in rooms
You've never been in

But time will show
Fame is yours
You cannot escape your fate
Publicity and immortality await
Many are here today
And will be forgotten tomorrow
But not you
Your journey is a different kind
Your calling is a special one
You have mountains to overcome
Oceans to conquer
And wars to fight
But you must fight them
Alone
And ask for nothing in return
Your glory awaits
That the task has been given to you
And you alone
Is both the gift and the reward
Not the acclaim
Not the praise
Not the applause
In time
We are all forgotten
But not you
You will be one of the greatest

And most amazing
Poets to ever have lived
This is who you are
Right here
And right now
Speak it
Be it
You are blessed
And all that live to see it.

INEVITABLY CHANGE COMES

After ten years
Even seven years
You're going to
Watch that person change
As you're changing
At one point
When you get married
You may even
Be at the same place
But then
Depending on
Who you are as people
You're both going to evolve
And change
And it's interesting
Seeing that change
And where it might veer off
Where you each veer off
Away from each other
As opposed to getting closer
Because they're growing
You're growing
Your brains are growing
Your experience of life

Is growing
What you want
Can change as well
As you get older
In your outlook
In your mind
And that can be affected
By things that happened
Years before you met
That forming
Of who you become
And where
You decide you want to go
And decide
That this isn't
What you want anymore
And drift away
That could have been
Something that was there
Before you even got married
Things are instilled
And your wants
And your needs
And your desires
Having children as well
That can alter

Your outlook on life
And change you
That's an important aspect
When the children grow up
And they're not dependent
On both of you anymore
Then they begin leaving
And you both
Have to come back
To yourselves
And then you start to see
The cracks
And the things
That don't align anymore
Or the cracks
Can be already there
But you're so busy
With the children
And everyday life
That you haven't had time
To focus on them
Until the children are gone
Then the cracks
Become more evident
And then it all begins
To fall in on itself.

IT'S A SAD, SAD PITY

It's a sad, sad pity
If you stay here
You'll become nothing
But a slave to a woman
It happens to every man
Irrespective of who they are
Or what they've known
Or where they come from
Or what they know
Or think they know
Despite their imagined coats of armour
Or all the defences they've created
Useless
And futile
She'll tear each down like paper
Like a good try
But not good enough
Like close, but no cigar
Effortlessly
As if the game was rigged
No win for him
There goes another again
Thrown into her den
Of manipulated men

It's a sad, sad pity
The men are turned to slaves
Criticism is the order of the day
And subservience, is the only way
The hunter, has become the prey
Under false pretence
Men stumble and fall
One after the another
For her cries of oppression
Only to share the same fate
Of their other male predecessors
Watching the mask fall off
Revealing the woman, the real oppressors
It's a sad, sad pity
She skilfully manipulates him
Step by step
To which he remains blind
Or at least, so he acts
From courtship to marriage
Blindly he pursues, until he is the catch
A victim to the trick
The rabbit in the hat
Fooled into believing
That there's something there
Besides the need for his resources
Time and care

She is now man of the house
He's just simply shares
It's a sad, sad pity
Man does all the work
And gets none of the praise
Father was never home
Is all the children say
When he finally returns
With the atlas on his back
And some hard earned treasure
He may be rewarded by the woman
With some brief sexual pleasure
It's a sad, sad pity
As always
Man is a slave to his desires
Chasing her
Like a carrot on a stick
Racing to the crack of her whip
And soon enough, dashes into her pit
To be used and abused by her
For however long she sees fit
It's a sad, sad pity
Man commits his life
To serving the woman
While the women compete
For which man they will keep

Like slave owners
She employs all means
To establish him as her property
Both him and his offspring
Even if she hasn't learned a thing
On how to do so properly
It's a sad, sad pity
The women are power hungry
And predatory
Egomaniacs
Caught up in themselves
And the anatomy of the male
Pushing idol theories about love
And romance, and male friends
That make no real sense
Even to themselves
They reject the patriarchy
For matriarchy
And pretend that it's going well
It's a sad, sad pity
The women are tricky
They say they are weaker
And so they need protecting
Which makes man the stronger sex
So they quickly reject it
Saying, we don't need a man

We can look after ourselves
In war, man is always ready
To die for the woman
Him and no-one else
But call on her to die for him
That man will hear only himself
It's a sad, sad pity
Men are trained
Like horses
For dating and courtship
Groomed, on short leashes
Denied sex, until whenever she pleases
And made to succumb
To her false charms, and needs
She trains and breaks him
Until he believes she made him
It's a sad, sad pity
Marriage is for women to celebrate
For her female family and friends to praise
To all gather and congratulate her
On successfully securing a slave
On a man's wedding day
He gives his independence away
He and his coalition of males
Give his freedom, a last goodbye wave
Knowing if he forsakes his new duties

For any number of days
He'll be exiled or shamed by society
Or even reported to the authorities
And locked away
It's a sad, sad pity
The government and society
Help the woman maintain rule
Over her freshly captured male slave
Her newly acquired fool
By keeping him in line
She who now legally owns
His liberty and his time
It's a sad, sad pity
The older women make sure
The younger ones are shown
How to properly tame the man
And be dominant in the home
He is trained very early
By his own mother
To rely on just her alone
To see domestic chores
Cooking, cleaning and laundry
As solely the woman's role
Thus in the kitchen
And in the bedroom
The woman maintains control

It's a sad, sad pity
The females breathe lies
To simply appease guys
Thus the young, dumb and naive
Come to believe
That which deceives the eyes
That witch sells a mind spell
And the mindless male buys
From her angled webs weaved
The wrangler has met her needs
Dangling threats whenever she speaks
He can never expect to be freed
Tangled helplessly in her weeds
And savagely from his flesh she feeds.

LIVING BETTER, FEELING GOOD

Life is good
I'm feeling in a really good place
Feeling really great
Lots of good things have happened
Since I spoke to you last
A few simple changes I've made
It's been for the better
Lots of good things
Small but major changes, for sure
On a life level
They're very major
Diet is a big one
My health and fitness in general
I eat a lot more fruit
And vegetables now
And salad
Fruit salad and vegetable salad
I cut out a lot of foods
That are not so good for me
Or anyone
I still have certain things
But I choose when I have it
I don't limit myself
To what I can have

I have everything I want
But I just choose
To have it at weekends
That type of thing
Not what I have
But when I have it
And by the time
The weekend comes around
I don't really fancy it as much
I don't go as crazy as I would
If I was doing it all week long
Eating whatever
At anytime
Like before
I'm now fasting as well
It does make you conscious
Of what you eat and don't eat
I eat much less
I do intermittent fasting
So I eat less
I eat in a smaller window
I eat now within
A six to eight hour window
I don't eat breakfast anymore
I won't eat until around twelve
Or one o'clock in the daytime

That'll be my first meal
My last meal will happen
Around seven
To eight o'clock
In the evening
I won't eat again
Until the next day
So I'm fasting
Sixteen to seventeen hours
The weekends
I just eat what I want
I don't go crazy
But I allow myself
To have the junk that I want
Because it's the only realistic way
That I'm going to be able
To sustain this new lifestyle
I don't like to call it diet
I like to call it lifestyle
Because diet implies
It's something
That's going to have an end
But lifestyle
Is more a new way of living
A new way of living
That I'm going to carry on living

A permanent change
A new direction in life
Also, I go to the gym now
Regularly
Five days a week
Yes, five days a week
I'm at the gym for sure
Minimum will be thirty minutes
On the treadmill, incline
I like to come out of the gym
Drenched in sweat
Completely soaking wet
That's how I like to feel
Feeling the heart pounding
That sets up my whole day
I feel amazing after that
I have lost weight too
I've trimmed down
People say it to me
They've noticed
That I've lost weight
My sister says
I look like I did
When I was younger
And I can see it too
I love it

And if anyone would know
Your sister would know, right
So it's a great thing
I can see it in the mirror
I feel better in my clothes
And everything
It's just amazing
Also, I made something
That I call miracle soil
Or I call it my magic mud
It's a concoction
That I made at home
It's another thing that I use now
It's a blend of
Really healthy natural ingredients
I put it on all my food
It just gives me this boost of energy
It's just amazing
A homemade
Natural remedy that I created
I took all of the ingredients
And I put them into my my blender
And blended it all up together
Into a fine powder
I put it all into small glass jars
And it stays in my food cupboard

I sprinkle that on my food
Any meals I have
I put it on my salad
Basically on most things I eat
You can put it in smoothies
You can have it as a hot drink
You could have it on a fruit salad
On your lunch or dinner
Any food you want to put it on
I recently
Put it on my fried egg croissant
It's just just a nice
Healthy something
To add to your plate, basically
So, that's another thing
That has me feeling great
I'm trying not have
Too much milk products
Eating much less dairy foods now
Because it's not too good for you
People wonder
Why they get bloated
And others
Are lactose intolerant
We're not supposed
To be consuming that stuff

I mean, I still like it
Because I eat ice cream
But our bodies are not designed
To have that in our system
We're not supposed
To drink cows milk
We're not calves
We're supposed to drink breast milk
From humans
And other natural sources of milk
From what grows from the earth
I don't know where
We got this whole thing from
But it's damaging us
And why we have
These reactions to it
Is because it's not good for us
It's not supposed to be
Something we eat
All this cheese
And all this milk
I remember this older lady
On the internet
I need to find her again
But she used to go around
And do these talks

Breaking down
How bad cows milk is for us
She described it as puss
She called it cow puss
I don't know
If she's still alive anymore
But she was really into that
She would explain
And break it all down
She definitely spoke a lot
About just how bad
Cows milk was for humans
And why we simply
Shouldn't be having it
I must look her up
And see if I can find her talks
They were very intelligent
And informative to me
At the time
I've never forgotten
Hearing her break it down
It doesn't sound like something
I want to be drinking or eating
But, you know
We grew up with milk, right
We grew up with this whole idea

That it's good for strong bones
And all this bullshit
We were taught
It's the complete opposite
You know, they say breakfast
Is the most important
Meal of the day
You know where that came from
I read a while ago
It came from the marketing
For a very well known
Popular brand
Of breakfast cereal
From nothing more
Than pure business strategy
They say that's where
That slogan came from
Just to make more people
Buy and eat cereal
But it's not true at all
It's not the most important
Meal of the day
I actually function
So much better now
Without breakfast
I also save a lot of time

Because I'm not thinking about
Prepping that morning meal
Or sitting down
To eat a morning meal
Or using up energy
Digesting that meal
So I have way more time
And I'm not tired
Because my body
Isn't trying to digest
What I ate
First thing in the morning
Before my system
Has even woken up
So that, that's a life changer
That's a game changer
Not having to worry
About breakfast
Or be slowed down
By breakfast in my system
Or needing to spend
Additional money
To accommodate
For that portion of food every day
So currently
My fast will start

From eight o'clock in the evening
Or seven
I will have my last meal for the day
By that time
And I won't eat again
Until around twelve
The next afternoon
That's a whole sixteen hours
I won't eat
Or eighteen
Depending on when I start
Or stop
I try to stick to that
Monday to Friday
Then Saturday and Sunday
I'll give myself a bit of freedom
To eat what I want
When I want
It's funny
How we look at the things
That are the worst for us
As treats
All the sugary crap
And junk food
That is going to clog the arteries
And encourage cancer

All this stuff
We we call it a treat
It's the wrong way
That we look at it
What I love now is
Because I'm getting into a routine
Of discipline
When it comes to my food
And because I'm fasting
Intermittent fasting
I only have a certain window
To eat within
So if food is around
And I'm fasting
That's it, I'm fasting
There's nothing
Anyone can tell me
They might say
Oh, have some of this
Oh, why don't you have some
I can just say No, I'm fasting
So it keeps me in line
It keeps me from over overeating
I'm thankful
To have that inner strength
Because there's many times

I could break down
And be weak
With people encouraging me
To eat things
Outside of my fasting window
And the wrong things
You have to be disciplined with it
Because there's only
One body we get
I'm sure there's a lot of people
Who are looking back
And they would make those changes
If it wasn't already too late
I'm around people like that
They just eat what they want
When they want
They're not bothered
About eating right
Or their future
Or health
Or exercise
I mean, they are
But they don't do anything
They're quite happy
Smoking
And eating

All types of food
At any time of the day
Drinking alcohol
All the time
I was like that, so I get it
Maybe there'll come a time
Where they either will change
Or they won't change
But I see it now
And I really
Want to make the changes
I've seen people
That haven't made the changes
And what they have to go through
In later life
Whether it's injecting themselves
Because they have diabetes
And ill health
Or someone
Who is literally
The only person
In their family
Who hasn't got diabetes
And they're making
Those life changes
And they've made

Such an amazing transformation
I've witnessed it
And it's made me
Want to change my life
And my habits
Different things
For different folks
But I know
That I've seen the light
And I want to make those changes
And I'm seeing the benefits as well
I used to be one of those people
That would bring cakes
Around people
And biscuits
And chocolate
I used to be the main person
At one point
For doing that
Encouraging everybody else
To eat sugar
Now, I'm the opposite
People have started
Being encouraged
To make changes
For better health

Because they're seeing me doing it
They've seen me lose weight
They've seen me feel better
Because I'm coming from the gym
They've seen what I'm eating
And I guess
It puts a mirror up
To themselves
And they think
They too
Should make changes
I hear that people have started
Getting on the exercise bike
At home
And saying
That they've started
Working out
And I've seen people
Bring less junk
And start eating better food more
I see them eating more vegetables
Where they would have had
A bag of crisps
They've now got carrot sticks
So I'm seeing people
Being influenced

By my changes
So it's reversing
I've cut down
My sugar intake
So I'm eating less
Of the refined sugar
The junk
The chocolate
The biscuits
The cakes
All of that
Even bread
Which also has sugar
Since I've cut out the sugar
I have way more energy
More than I've experienced
In years
I have so much more energy
And so check this out
I'm eating less food
Which they say is fuel
And energy, right
And I'm eating less sugary things
They say sugar
Gives you energy, right
And I have way more energy

Than I've had in years
I have to stop myself
From jumping on tables
Because it just
Wouldn't be appropriate
Out in public
Or in the office
Or in a cafe, or something
I just feel
I've got so much energy
I feel like just
Jumping on a chair sometimes
Sometimes
I randomly start dancing
For seemingly no reason
That's just how I feel
Energised and excited
I haven't felt like that in years
It's almost like I'm high
It's amazing
And this is just
Through fasting
Cutting out
Certain refined junk
And the gym
Exercise

This is what I have to eat
Pretty much on a regular basis
I'll have a bowl
Of green leafy spinach
Add to that
A hard boiled egg, mashed
Some black olives
I add some kind of meat
Like shredded duck
Or turkey strips
Or chicken breast pieces
Add to that
Raw mixed nuts
With raisins
And then
My miracle soil on top
And some light salad dressing
Like honey and mustard
I have that all together
As a meal
Mixed in one bowl
I'll have that
And really enjoy it
That's one of my main staple meals
That's what I'll break my fast with
On a day to day basis

I'll have that ready to go
Always some kind of salad
With mainly perhaps spinach
Or some kind of mixed greenery
I'm going to start cutting down
On the meat side of it, I think
And just have it
Without any meat
It's all a new work in progress
We'll see
But for sure
I am feeling and looking
One hundred percent
Better than ever
I'm building it
Into a sustainable lifestyle
An ongoing habitual lifestyle
That will undoubtedly
Add vigour
Vitality
Youth
And years to my life.

LOVE FLOW

You have to be
The most amazing woman
I've ever met
From head to toe
You're beautiful
Like a warm night
Star gazing
Under the moon
Here we are
Wrapped up together
In a feeling
In a mood
And this is truly
The best place
On earth
To be right now
Who knew
That we would eventually
Find one another
And become lovers
The dream seemingly deferred
But not in vain
And despite the pain
It was worth the wait, all the same

In a warm embrace
We hold each other
And the air sounds like music
Young children playing
Well into the night
As the streets cars drive by
And it just feels right
I'm vibing to the tune of you
And you're doing
Just the same with me too
We are one
Who knew
The day like this would come
The world feels amazing right now
And fun
This is one of those nights
That you just know will end well
Not a thing to worry for
Only to enjoy more
And if there's a worry
It's only that it all ends too soon
Those nights like this
These are the ones
You want to last forever
And never end
Days you wish you could just replay

Again and again
And we'd be
Completely fine with that
Lost away in our own world
A world of our own
Nowhere to be
Nowhere to go
Just holding each other
And letting love flow.

MISSING SHOES

He came in the door from work
The same old way he always does
Laboured and exhausted looking
But slightly more tired than usual
He threw his cap off somewhere
In his usual nonchalant way
And as he sat down
At the kitchen table with us
We noticed he was holding
An old pair of women's shoes
He sighed a deep sigh
Said he didn't understand women
Just imagine, he said
It's an hour before
You have to wake up for work
Your girlfriend calls your phone
Wakes you up to tell you
It's over between you
Totally caught off guard
And half asleep
You ask her why
She says she's tired
Fed up of the relationship
That she doesn't see a future with you

And that she needs some time apart
I was silent for a minute, he said
I then took a quiet deep breath
Cleared my throat a little
And with a calm voice
I said to her, Okay, fine
If that's what you want
Thirty minutes later
I was at her house
I collected these shoes
That I bought for her
On her birthday
Just over two months ago
Don't they look old, he said
It's because she wears them
Every single day to work
And back again
And outside of work
To the shops
To parties
To visit family
Even walking the dog
Through the park
She loves these shoes
I took them, he said
Because I bought her them

I took these shoes
Because I know
They are the only thing
She will miss, concerning me.

MY DREAM GIRL

Well
You see
The thing is
I met this girl
She was like a dream
Walking in that room
I just didn't know what to do
Or what to say
It was like, wow
I've never seen a woman
Move so beautifully
So graceful
Her blouse
Her skirt
And little kitten heels
She had her hair tied back
She was just there
I couldn't even concentrate
On what I had to do
She was just, wow
She was amazing
I've never seen a girl like that
I have never seen a girl like that
Outside of my dreams

She wasn't real
I woke up
In my bed
In my home
And I was alone
She didn't exist
Outside of that dream
She didn't exist at all
My mind had created her
In my sleep
And that was the only place
We were ever going to meet.

NEXT BOOK

So, she said
My honest opinion
Our date went great
Was incredible
Was magical
Perfect
Great conversation
And great sex
However, she said
When a couple of weeks passed
Without a call
Without a proper message
Without a hope
It seemed
Like a choreographed game
It took me back
To my twenties
I don't know, she said
If you intended it or not
Anyway
It doesn't matter
I will still remember you finely
But some advice
In the future

When you meet someone
That you consider special
Make sure, she advised
That you take the time
To show interest
To show that you care
Because it's fifty-fifty
At least
For anything healthy
And worth it
Books are just that, books
And if you feel
You'd rather
Use the time for a book
It's because that someone
Is not that special
Anyway, she said
I repeat
I will remember you finely
And I hope
That everything goes well
With your books
And your art
And creativity
Much love.

ORGASM SHOP & BODY SWAP

She said she wishes
She could be a man
Just for a day
Just so she could experience
What it's like to be male
To know what it's like
To be in a masculine body
To feel what it's like
To have sex with a woman
I responded
I would love to be a woman
For a day
Just to see
What these orgasms
Are all about
That women experience
Differently from men
They look great
These multiple orgasms
And being able to keep going
No matter how many times
You've orgasmed
For men
It's that one height

Of ejaculation
And then
We're coming down from there
Whereas the woman is ready
To have the same again
These multiple orgasms
This whole sensation throughout
Whereas the man
Is going somewhere
He's going up to a peak
And then that's it
Once he gets there
But the woman
Can keep peaking
I would love to experience that
To feel what that's like
I told her
Maybe we should swap
You could be me
I can be you
We'd just swap for a day
You can go out as me
And I'll go out as you
And we'll have fun
And we'll explore that
This is all purely about sex

This is just
Solely for the pleasure
For the sexual activity
We don't even need
To leave the room
We'd just use each other
But I'm you
And you're me
I'm swapping
To experience it as me
But in your body
With the way
Your body works
And vice versa
There's nothing else going on
Except me
Being able to feel
What you feel
When you enjoy yourself
As a woman
And I get to feel that
I get to feel
Those multiple orgasms
And you get to feel
What it's like
For a man to do it

She said
We can squirrel ourselves away
I can be her
She can be me
And we can just
Have sex
All day long
I said, Yes
Or until we're satisfied
But I don't know
How long
You'd be able to go
Being the man
She said, I could tell her
How much she could take
I explained
Your body would tell you
You're experiencing it as me
So it's whatever
You're going to be able to do
As a man
You're going to be doing that
Whatever you can manage
And vice versa
She said, you never know
With artificial intelligence

And virtual reality
With time
We might be able to swap
In some way
I said, Yeah
I don't know how, though
But yeah
I'm sure in the future
We'll all be doing just that
And more.

PLEASE CHECK YOUR OWN LUGGAGE

I think this idea
Of someone
Who's in their fifties
Saying to someone else
Of similar age
That they don't want
Anyone with baggage
Sounds crazy
When you think about it
Because I really don't think
You could exist
Anywhere on the planet
And not acquire
Some form of baggage
Even if you didn't have children
From a previous relationship
You didn't have a messy divorce
Or you weren't raped
Or sexually abused
Or didn't suffer
A traumatic childhood
Or go through some tragedy in life
That affected you mentally
And psychologically

Had zero negative experiences
Or anything
Generally considered baggage
I still don't think it's possible
That you would come to someone
With absolutely no baggage
It would just simply
Be more a case of
What is your particular type
Or brand of baggage
It's not do you have any
It's what type do you have
Because we all have some
And the size and weight
Of the luggage we have
Is subjective
Based on who's seeing it
Just because of
The way of the world
The nature of existence
And being a human being
The world beats you up regardless
And hands you your bags
Irrespective
Of the relationships you've had
Or haven't had

And even the lack
Of those things
The lack of having a partner
Or marriage
Or children
Would beat you up as well
That in itself
Would come with things
The fact
That you haven't gone that road
There would be other things
That you would have experienced
On that road
Or taken on
Or suffered
That would add baggage to you
In some psychological way
Even a virgin has baggage
So someone who's been on earth
For a total of fifty years
Saying to someone else
That they don't want to be
With a person with baggage
Who may happen
To have children
And has had

A few failed relationships
That didn't work out
Sounds crazy to me
Because they themselves
Have baggage
They might not
Recognise it that way
But no-one alive
Comes without baggage
Not even a newborn baby
Children are often
Born into baggage
Based on certain circumstances
Outside of their control
As they say
You can't choose your parents
Everyone
Has some type of baggage
And there might be
A thousand types
By the age of fifty
If not long before
You'll definitely
Have some 'baggage'
Of your own
That you're carrying around

Whether knowingly
Or unknowingly
When it comes to relationships
And other people's baggage
You'll just have to
Carefully choose
Which type of baggage
And how much
You're actually willing
And able to handle
But either way
You should definitely
Check your own luggage
Before criticising
Or finding fault
With someone else's.

PROVIDENCE

May you
continuously
bring forth

Things
that you never
have to force

Things
that flow easily
to you

As if
they were
always yours.

RAISED BY AN ARTIST

She was raised
By an artist, she said
A man who had to be creative
Every day
A great writer
But too critical
And his work
Went into the fire most times
But his paintings survived
Even when he had no money
For materials
He found a way
Once he made a portrait
Of her brother, she recalls
From two colours
On a piece of plywood
He put yellow down
And then covered it
With brown
And etched the image
With a nail
She said, after he died
She made a website of his work
He was well unique

In his personality
Eccentric
Stubborn
With an infectious laugh
He could be difficult
As he took up all the space
In the room
And was kind of dominant
But also very empathetic
And kind
She brought any troubled friends
That she had, to him
And he would adopt them
He just had to be
Making something
Various rooms in the house
Would be transformed
And walls knocked down
A huge studio emerged
In the former kitchen
And dining room
And a little porch
Turned into a new kitchen
A portrait
Became a landscape
Became an abstract

For many years
He painted this way
And the canvas
Was thick with paint
No matter what
He was always working
On a number of things
He was a total character
I said, he reminds me
Of myself in many ways
To which she replied
Then maybe
I and her will click
He and I got along well
For the most part, she said
He fully expected me
To be a sculptor
He thought I was like him
But I was afraid
Of being that eccentric.

RAPING OF THE INNOCENTS

He still doesn't talk about it much
Though I can always clearly see
That it still affects him to this day
Despite all of the therapy sessions
He always sounds to me
Like someone in a state of shock
Whenever he talks about it
Which isn't too often
And it's never like an injured person
Looking to others wanting sympathy
But more to be helpful in the world
As if saving a mother and her unborn child
From potential harm
Or like obstructing a vehicle in the street
So an old lady can safely cross the road
Or rescuing an animal trapped somewhere
He seems to offer this voice from a place
That hopes the experience he suffered
Doesn't happen to someone else
He was twenty-eight years old
And in a really terrible way
He'd found himself destitute and homeless
And living rough on the streets of London
Through drug addiction

It was a constant daily struggle
One like you could never imagine
He recalls
A group of black men and women
Looking after and taking care of him
They made sure he was never alone
Giving him items
That they themselves needed
Things like blankets
He became a part of their community
But his battles with addiction
Led him to join the company of others
That provided him with alcohol or drugs
All the while knowing deep down
That he was being disloyal
To those helping him
And keeping him safe
He at some point met this white woman
Who he thought was a saviour princess
Even at twenty-eight
He can't believe how naive he was
She bought him
A gigantic bottle of whisky
And gave him a cellphone
With a contract SIM card
He didn't once believe

That it was all part of a plan
He never even considered it
He thought she liked him
Ridiculous, he says, looking back now
Knowing what a mess he was in
For about a week
She let him stay at her place
It was nearby to a car repair centre
Nothing untoward was happening
She was just looking after him
One night, she invited him to a 'party'
Which he was excited to go to
He had slowed his drinking down
During that week
And was fully sober and clear minded
When she picked him up to take him
He was sitting in her off-white BMW
And while on their way
She says, my friends like you
Just have sex with them
He replied
That her friends had never met him
And laughed it off
As his mind was far more fixated
On the alcohol in store for him
And the great time he was about to enjoy

He was offered a drink
As soon as he arrived
The house was full
Of white men and women
And boys and girls
He didn't know the significance
At the time
But these girls and boys
Were all black
And extremely young
He saw them
Being led upstairs by women
But again, didn't connect the dots
He had hardly drank any of his drink
When some 'coke'
Was offered to him first
Again, he couldn't believe his luck
Cocaine too, he rejoiced inside himself
He snorted the biggest line
That one could imagine
The women on the sofa opposite
Were telling him to go ahead
And have more
Which he didn't decline
The last thing he remembers
After this moment

And before having
Any more of the drink
He was feeling the need to sleep
He remembers the woman
That had brought him
Taking him upstairs into a room
And lying down in bed
Putting the cellphone she gave him
Under the pillow
Which he always did, and still does
And that was it
He was gone, into a deep sleep
It was about six to seven hours later
When the day was just beginning
That he came around
To find two very old white men
Asking him to 'let them finish'
And something about 'really quick'
Him being naturally rebellious
His inner rebel kicked into gear
And he screamed out
He shouted out
And made the biggest commotion
The woman that had taken him there
Suddenly appeared in the room
And he was dragged and slapped

And thrown into a bathtub
Which resulting in crying
And a feeling of despair
Like he'd never known
He remembers
Being ordered out of the bath
He found his clothes
That had been removed
In his unconsciousness
And got himself dressed
His cellphone was gone
One of the men's trousers
Were on the floor
He searched through the pockets
To steal any money he could find
To get him back to London
And to the police
But only found a driver's licence
Which he took
He then ran out from the house
Still shouting and screaming
As loud as he could
To deter them from coming after him
After a while, exhausted
He collapsed
Outside a nearby convenience store

They helped him to get a taxi cab
And from there
He went to the police station
He was in such an awful state
That he was sent directly to the hospital
And as with all such cases
He went through hours of examination
He'd handed over to them
The driver's licence he'd taken
For his wellbeing they placed him
In safe temporary accommodation
And made sure that he stayed
By checking in on him daily
Unfortunately, the case went no further
Because of a 'lack of evidence'
He believes, due to his situation
And his unfavourable presentation
At the time
That no-one would believe him anyway
He was addicted to alcohol and homeless
Says he will never forget
Those boys and girls
And the sadness he saw in them
Never ever
Or the men, and how old they were
And the women

And how nice they appeared at first
A few years later
He saw one of the men
On the news
He had been caught and jailed
For grooming children
And threatening young boys with a gun
If they didn't let him have sex with them
He says he doesn't even know
If the same man had his way with him
During the seven hours
That he was unconscious
From the drug they'd given him
What he says he does know
Is that it was all planned out
And was taking place in huge numbers
That it has been going on for years
And it is rampant in cities
All across the country
This is the reason why
People are so angry, and afraid
But not everyone gets to see it
It's easy to just watch the news
And see and hear stories
That don't reflect the true horror
Of what's going on, he says

It's easy not to really relate
But he has experienced the rough end
That has gone unchecked
And ignored for so many years
We have communities
That will never ever comprehend
Or be able to appreciate these issues
And the fear that there is
Of seeing children
Being approached
In broad daylight
In the street
Out in public places
Being filmed and videoed
And taken photos of
On stranger's camera phones
Being groomed and coerced
Drugged and raped
Lured into sordid bedrooms
Sexually assaulted and abused.

REGARDING THE SEARCH

I'm not looking

For anything

As much as

I'm looking around

I've called off the search

Letting it find me

This time around

By putting myself

In the places

Where I can be found.

STYGIAN

Let us pray
There's no hope
There are no soulmates
There is no right one
Only the one right now
Or no-one
Run
They're trying to kill us
Please let us out
Why is it so dark down here
Because it's dark down here
This is all your fault
Where's your father
Sex is a temporary currency
Run
They only love you when you're dead
The devil wouldn't survive here
What was that
That sound
What was that
You're not a human being
You're a virus
They value a dog's life more than yours
Run

Attention whore
You're insecure
Irrational
You're mentally unstable
It's all in your fucking head
Let us pray
There's no hope
There are no soulmates
There is no right one
Only the one right now
Or no-one
Run
They're trying to kill us
Please let us out
Why is it so dark down here
Because it's dark down here
This is all your fault
Where's your father
Sex is a temporary currency
Run
They only love you when you're dead
The devil wouldn't survive here
What was that
That sound
What was that
You're not a human being

You're a virus
They value a dog's life more than yours
Run
Attention whore
You're insecure
Irrational
You're mentally unstable
It's all in your fucking head
Let us pray
There's no hope
There are no soulmates
There is no right one
Only the one right now
Or no-one
Run
They're trying to kill us
Please let us out
Why is it so dark down here
Because it's dark down here
This is all your fault
Where's your father
Sex is a temporary currency
Run
They only love you when you're dead
The devil wouldn't survive here
What was that

That sound
What was that
You're not a human being
You're a virus
They value a dog's life more than yours
Run
Attention whore
You're insecure
Irrational
You're mentally unstable
It's all in your fucking head.

TEARS BY THE LAKE

Grand risings, she said
Sending you love
And that yesterday
She went to the lake
And it was so beautiful
How she stood there
Beside the lake
And listened
To my spoken word
Which was so powerful
That it actually made her cry
Particularly 'The Next Level'
I don't think
It could have resonated
Any more powerfully
If it had tried, she recalled
It was like, Oh my God
I just think it's so amazing
How we get given gifts
And knowledge
And power
Or wisdom
Through spoken word
Through other people

Through things
That have been done
A while ago
But just seem
So incredibly potent
And literally
Like it was just written
For me in that moment
So thank you, she said
Very very much
I truly enjoyed
And was deeply moved
And it got my brain thinking
Which is what
It's all supposed to do, right
So thank you very much
She said, once again
Sending you lots of love
On this beautiful sunny day.

THE CALLING

I feel things
They come to life so perfectly
Through moments
Through people
With emotion
I transfer it all to the page
I write about it
Turn it into art
All I need is myself
My soul
I feel
And I see the truth
All in my brain
I never try to feel it
But I always want to feel it
And it comes
Through openness
Through stillness
I've always felt it
Even when I feel nothing
I feel it all the time
Not just sometimes
And I'm held there
Captured

Enveloped inside my mind
Feeling it in my soul
I really do
Summoning me to write it
To share the feeling
The thought
The sentiment
That energy
From where it came
With force
Through words
On a page
From a voice
Inside
Calling
Needing to be heard
And I hear it
And feel it
Sometimes I'm staring
But I'm not looking at anything
Not listening
In those moments
I'm not here
I'm there
Heeding the calling
I'm taken away from this place

Into a weird
And warped other space
Most people find me strange
There's something different
That they can't figure out
Insane to some
Who can't understand
A cause for concern
But it's where the art comes from
All of that
Those spaces in-between
Between freak
Between genius
Between being the quiet one
Between ruining things
Memories
People
I chose to be born
Had to come and see
See it all play out
I remember
Knowing the outcome
Before it came to be
I always did
And was right
I was always ahead

Now I just want to see more
Remember more
Access more
Sometimes
The frequencies overlap
Get crossed
And it's harder to see
To listen
To hear
To make sense of it all
The clarity comes
In the stillness
That's why it's so important
To quiet the loudness
With silence
So in the dark
Amidst the noise
I can hear
And I can feel.

THE OLD SALOON CAR

Kids like to conform
With their peers, she said
And rebel
Against their parents
They lived in LA
And didn't have a car
She was about eight
Her dad had built a sidecar
On his bicycle
That fit all three of them
But the other kids
Always talked
About their parents cars
So she begged him
To get them one
He had quit his job at UCLA
And was trying to support them
With his art
And writing alone
No money for a car
But that week
He came home
With a 1940s saloon
Told her to get in

And asked her
Where do you want to go
She said by the school
So all the kids could see
We had a car too
She said she had no clue
It wasn't a fine car
So they did
And it made it back home
And died
Then they were the only kids
With a play car
In their yard
She was happy.

THE STARTING LINE

My mother used to write
She got me into writing
Quite early on
It was really important to her
That I wrote and spoke well
And had a good command
Of the English language
She was concerned
That I did well in that area
In school
Also, I had gone to Barbados
And lived there for a few years
And went to school there
She wanted me to
Have that experience
That she had growing up
Coming from Barbados
So sent me to live there
With my grandmother
And great grandmother
When I eventually
Came back to England
I had a Bajan accent
And had picked up

The local slang and twang
And spoke very differently
To how I'd left England
She didn't want that
To go against me
So she was very proactive
In having me write
And speak 'properly'
So I started re-learning
All over again
As it was before I'd left
Making sure
That I was at the top in school
In writing and spelling
So that opened up
That creative door
With regards to writing
I was always interested
In words
In language
And literature
And stories
So that was already there
And so
That was an early introduction
To the writing

Also my drawing
Because she used to paint
She used to watch Bob Ross
On television
And then she would paint along
So that's where
My drawing influences came in
That was from
A very early age as well
I used to draw a lot
In pencil
And felt tip colouring pens
For a while
I did a lot of drawing
I got really good at it
To the point
People didn't believe it was me
I remember at one point
I was in a children's hospital
And the nurses didn't believe
That I did the drawings
That they were seeing
I remember my mother
Being annoyed at that
Because I did draw them
She didn't like that

But that was how
My creative journey developed
I was always that way, always
I can't remember a time I wasn't
It makes me think about
How much nurture plays
In regards to talent, maybe
What influences we have around us
As well as nature
I was always creating, always
And it has stayed with me
To write
I don't know any other way
I didn't start out wanting to do it
As far as I know
But then maybe I did
Maybe from a deep desire
To express things
To communicate something
Maybe that's why
We're here now, as a result
In this conversation
I do know
It just came naturally to me
And it's remained
That same way 'til this day

It just came very natural to me
To do it
I started it
As a way of expression
Because I was the only child
For quite a while
Definitely for the first
Twelve years of my life
Living as an only child
And by the time you get to twelve
You've been an only child
For the majority
Of your childhood years
Even if you have
Brothers and sisters
That come afterwards
So it was just my way of living
When I just wanted to play
And explore, and draw
And do creative things
That's what I did
So it wasn't something
I necessarily wanted to do
It's just how I came up
It was just in me
To do those things

And they just followed me
On into adult life
They were always
My go-to things then
And they still are now
I just get something from it
But I didn't have it as a dream
To be a writer
To be creative
It's just the thing
That I get something from
I guess
I always will at this point
I'd say for sure
I feel like
I'm meant to be doing it
I was asked
If I could change what I do
To do something else
Would I
And the answer is
I wouldn't
Would I change it
To do something else
Like a pilot
Or an astronaut

Or a zookeeper
No
I like being a writer
And a poet
And every day
I like to feel
That I'm becoming
A better and better one
I like that pursuit
I picture it like this
I'm passionate about it
Like a racing car driver
That's the first thing
That came to my mind
They want to, obviously
Beat what they've done
What they've achieved
On the track
Their speed
The way they
Handle the vehicle
The wins
They want to improve
They want to do better
The next time
And get stronger

And better
And faster
That's how I think about it
That's how I feel
About what I do
I don't see myself
Doing anything else
I don't want to do anything else
I just want to
Break my own records
That's how I feel.

TO SOMETHING GREAT

How's it going over there
New book, she asked me
Much has happened
Since we last spoke
She said
I felt quite frustrated
About the way I waited
And wanted
And clearly
You were in a different place
I got so much inspiration
And spark, she told me
From connecting with you
And then a lot of frustration
So I thought
It's better to break contact
Interestingly enough
My strong desire
Has moved on eventually
Very fascinating
How that hooks
On certain things
In your case, she said
The creative mind

It's like there was a part
That needed to unlock
In me, she explained
And that opened
In connection with you
And I then connected
The need to be with you
To that somehow
And there is something
Inherently fascinating
In a man
Who is so dedicated
To something great
That seems to be
A common thread for me
I really like that, she added
And then I get frustrated
But I'm like that too
And I know
I have frustrated men
For never being
My number one in life
Anyhow, she said
Let me know
What's up
If you want to connect

Or what
As long as we are clear
She said
And honest with each other
I'm cool.

TODAY I THOUGHT ABOUT FRANK

They said
He left work that day
That evening, or afternoon
And said, see you tomorrow
And went home as usual
It was said
That he'd had an argument
With his girlfriend
And that same night
That he took a bunch of pills
And went to bed
And didn't wake up
In the morning
And then, of course
He hadn't turned up
That morning to work
That he'd taken an overdose
And that he was
No longer with us
I remember being called aside
To be told the news
I as I was one of
The people he knew
And I guess

You could say
Was close to
Or at least
That people were aware
That I was one of the people
That he spoke to
On a fairly regular basis
I had no idea though
That he used to be a she
I mean, not that it matters
Not that it mattered then
Or not that it matters now
But I just never knew
And I only found out
After he'd left us
I just thought
He was a really effeminate boy
I didn't realise that he
Was born a female
And had gone through changes
I can't imagine what that's like
Or what that would have been like
For me say, if I was twenty-seven
And my family didn't agree with it
And all the things
That come with being different

I guess that part
I can relate to
Just the being different
In the world
I remember him
Bringing up
Some chocolates for me
That had been left by a customer
Who wanted to say thank you
For the help I'd given them
They had been delivered
To the ground floor
Reception desk
And as that's where
Frank was often stationed
He brought them upstairs
To where I was
It's just little things
You remember
I still keep the note
That he or whoever
Wrote and attached
On the box of chocolates
I don't know
Who wrote the note
If it was him or someone else

The chocolates
Are no more, obviously
But the note I've kept
Because of its attachment
To the memory of him
It had my name on it
And where it was to be delivered to
And to it, I later added
In Loving Memory
of Frank Williams
That's the only physical thing
I have of his memory
I've taped it to my desk
Because he was a nice guy
He was someone you remember
For being a likeable person
And I guess the shock of it
This young person
Is just suddenly
Not with us anymore
That's just crazy
So, yeah, I kept that note
Another memory
I have of him
Is he was dating
And seeing someone

I think he was deciding
Where to go
What to eat
Where he should take them
For a meal
That was cool
So we talked about that
With some others
And we all gave some suggestions
That's another memory
I have of him
That I look back fondly upon
You just never know
How precious
Those moments are going to be
When someone
Is not around anymore
I think we take these interactions
Very often for granted
They're not really that special
They are, but then
They're so much more special
When someone suddenly dies
It stays with you
And every so often
I see his face

And his mannerisms
And hear his voice
What a cool cat, man
They say, sometimes
It's always the most cheerful
Easy-going
Seemingly go lucky
No care in the world
Kind ones
That are taken from us
In some way
Or at least, those are the ones
That we never suspected
Anything
Could possibly be wrong with
They're the ones we least expect
Are suffering somehow inside
Silently
Those are seemingly
The strong ones
Who we couldn't imagine
Are going through turmoil inside
And feeling so bad
That they might want
To not be alive anymore
That something

From an argument with someone
Could trigger that desire in them
To just want to end their life
It just goes to show
You never know
What's going on with a person
No matter
What you see on the outside
No matter what they show
No matter
What you think you know
Sometimes
You just never really know
Sometimes, they themselves
May never even really know
What's going on with themselves
Until something triggers them
And that switch goes off in them
And that's the last straw for them
And they had no idea themselves
That they'd be feeling that way
From one day
Feeling the complete opposite
To the next day
Feeling like, fuck it
I'm out of here

I heard he was really doing well
In his new position
That he was very liked
And that he was
Being promoted
And rising
Up the ranks, you could say
In a short space of time
I have no doubt
He was talented guy
Because he had
That energy about him
Sometimes
You just take to people
With a vibe
An energy
A spirit
Something they have
That you're drawn to
And it's when you hear
That someone like that
Is suddenly gone
It's a shock
It's been a while now
Since his passing
But every so often

Something someone says
Something I see
Reminds me of that boy
Gone too soon
Twenty-seven
Is way too soon to go
You're always left
With so many questions
And not many answers
Because the person
The one person
Who can answer them
Is not here to answer them
I guess all that's left
Is to celebrate
Celebrate the good memories
The good times
The laughs
All the good things
As well as a good person
In pain
Who is now
Free
No longer in pain
Rest well, Frank
No more pain.

UNTIL THEN

I had to let you go
Maybe I'll see you
Sometime down the road
You're not the one for me
And not everybody knows
But I do
That's just the way it goes
Maybe you didn't understand
Or fully comprehend
I'm leaving this here
And moving on ahead
Please know
I meant everything I said
Perhaps organically
Somehow
Someplace
If it's meant to be
Our paths will meet again
Either way
I hope this reaches you
And if so
I leave you until then.

VOLUNTEERING WITH MET POLICE

I enjoy volunteering
With the Metropolitan Police
Engaging with communities
And providing
Reassurance on the streets
We patrol local areas
While conducting weapon sweeps
We help make safer neighbourhoods
By being present
And putting residents at ease
We are also a part of the bustling
And busy night time economy
Encouraging the public to keep safe
And act and think responsibly
We volunteer to help the Police
Deter criminal activities
Whilst being a friendly face
Working in partnership with the Met
To help make London
A much safer and better place.

WHERE DID I GO

She asked
Where I'd gone
Where did I go
The man that woke her
From a torpor
On that soporific day
Who burrowed
Into her head
And fired up her thoughts
Until they shimmied
Like ants
On an overheated walkway
Whose frankness
Shocked and soothed her
All at once
Her sigh releasing
At the recognition
Of a like-minded brother
Whose sexiness was overt
Not covert
Making her want to open
Not close her door
Whose laughter
Was infectious

And fed hers
Fuel to the flame
Of her often
Lop-sided brain
Where did I go
Was I just
An afternoon's dream.

WHY I'M ON A DATING APP

First of all, I'm single
I live happily by myself alone
But at times, occasionally
I like being with someone
I like actual human connection
I like in person conversation
I like physical chemistry
I like feminine energy
I like femininity around me
I like intimacy
I like warmth
I like touch
I'm there because
I'm a guy
I'm a man
I'm a male
Hot blooded
Simply a human
With human needs
Just like the rest of the species
Who are programmed to eat
Biologically designed to feast
It makes sense to be there
Even non-single people flock there

Hunting for something
New to taste
Looking for prey
And taking up space
That's just how it is nowadays
That's where you'll find
Everyone's face
You can't even really approach
Women on the street anymore
Because first of all
Her face is in her phone
And no matter
How good looking you are
Nowadays, it's like
Why are you talking to me
It's that confused
Suspicious
Annoyed look of
What are you approaching me for
Sadly, it's an unusual
And strange thing to do now
Because everyone's so used to
Communicating through a screen
So, it's the place to be now
In that regard
If you want to get someone's attention.

WOMAN SUFFERS HEART ATTACK

On the way home today
After my Logistics Support
Volunteer shift
I sat on a bench by a bus stop
Ten minutes walk
From our East London
Ambulance Hub
Taking in the evening sunshine
And people watching
A bus pulled up at the bus stop
It stayed there a few minutes
As buses do
And I just assumed
It was to regulate the service
As is often normal with buses
It was there a while
And I took no notice of it
Just continued
Enjoying the sunshine and sea
I'm joking, there was no sea
After realising
The bus
Had been parked there
A while longer

Than one would expect
For a few minutes
Of service regulation
It dawned upon me
That the bus
Had been there so long
That everyone
Who was on the bus
Had disembarked
To continue their journey
Via another bus
Or by other means
The bus had emptied
And the back doors
Remained open
Still onboard the bus
I saw the driver
Pacing back and forth
A woman sitting
At a window seat
Near the front
And a man
Wearing a high visibility vest
Also pacing back and forth
Whilst talking on his phone
I then noticed the driver

Bending down
Talking to the seated woman
Who was now leaning forward
It appeared
Something wasn't right
So I boarded the bus
To see
If there was anything wrong
And if I could possibly
Offer any help
I quickly learned
Both the driver
And the man on his phone
Were each communicating
With the emergency services
Trying to get an ambulance
To come to her aid
The bus driver told me
That the woman
Who was now leaning
Against the window
Holding her chest
And seemingly in a lot of pain
Said to him
That she's having a heart attack
And that she had one last week

And that's how she knew
What was wrong with her
Still holding her chest
Saying she needed the hospital
And she doesn't want to die
She managed to present
Some medication
From her bag to me
The man on his phone
Was at this time
Still giving information
About her condition
To the emergency services
The bus driver
Was also doing the same
From his driver seat
As she was still sitting
And leaning over
But now
Not making any movement
I spoke to her
And she responded
I then just kept talking to her
And tried to keep her calm
I asked her name
Which she told me

I had a look at her medication
And reassured her
Help is on the way
While she told me
Some of what the bus driver
And the other man present
Had already told me she'd said
Prior to my arrival
I decided to call the Hub directly
And told them
What was happening
To see if there were any
Ambulance crews available
That could immediately assist
It seemed like
A good ten mins had passed
While waiting
For any ambulance to arrive
The man was still on his phone
And the driver
Was also on a call
Trying to get emergency assistance
I don't know
What made me look
Out of the bus window behind me
At this moment

But I turned around
And saw an ambulance
Driving past
In the opposite direction of the bus
It was a St John Ambulance
I recognised it was Peter and Shelbie
Just on their way to the Hub
To begin their twilight shift
For the evening
They had no idea
There was an emergency situation
Taking place inside the bus
On the other side of the road
I immediately ran out of the bus
And managed to flag them down
Signalling them to come to the bus
I perhaps could've done a better job
Of displaying urgency
Panic and distress
And an emergency help required now
Type of energy
As afterwards
I learned
That they initially thought
I was just waving at them
To say hello

Nevertheless
On went the blue lights
And they turned around
And came back
And parked in the road
Behind the bus
And jumped out
To find out what the matter was
I informed them
That a woman on the bus
Says she's having a heart attack
How long we'd been there
Gave them her medication
And made them aware
That she'd been given
Some water to drink
Just prior by the bus driver
And that she informed us
She'd suffered a heart attack
Just last week
They hastily grabbed a Lifepak
From the ambulance
An oxygen cylinder bag etc
And boarded the bus
To aid the woman
As they were talking to her

And carrying out their observations
In between
The cramped seating area
Of the bus and the stairway
The woman began
To vomit profusely
I ran out of the bus
And onto to the ambulance
And brought back sick bags
And tissues
And gave a sick bag to the woman
After vomiting
The woman when asked
Said she was unable
To walk to the ambulance
She was then placed
In a carry chair
And hurriedly wheeled off the bus
By the crew
Towards the ambulance
Just as this was happening
London Ambulance Service
Turned up with their ambulance
And parked up behind ours
As Peter and Shelbie
Hadn't signed on for work yet

And were without an airwave radio
The woman
Was then handed over
To the LAS instead
To be transported from there
To the hospital
As this was happening
I had collected the Lifepak
Its leads
And oxygen cylinder bag
From the bus
And took them back
Onto our ambulance
I placed the Lifepak
Back in its bracket
And then
I Clinell wiped clean the leads
On realising when I touched them
That, like the other equipment
They hadn't quite fully escaped
The shower of projectile vomit
The bus had received
I further wiped my hands clean
And placed the used wipes
In the clinical waste bin
At the back of the ambulance

By this time
Peter and Shelbie
Had returned
From handing over the woman
To the LAS
We were still parked in the road
There was right then
A moment we somehow
All at the same time
Were walking down
The ramp of the ambulance
Exiting the open back doors
I looked up to see
Another St John Ambulance crew
Driving past us
On their way
To another emergency call
They smiled
And acknowledged us
As they drove by
In that very moment
I felt ten feet tall
And I felt proud
Walking out
Of that ambulance today
I felt like one of three heroes

I feel useful
I feel like
I'm a part of something
Meaningful
Making a difference
Today, although unexpected
Unplanned and unscheduled
Marks my first ever 'event'
As a St John Ambulance First Aider.

WOMAN WALKS INTO A BAR

Eve rang me one evening
While she was walking her dog
We talked for a while
About this, about that
We talked about books
And her penchant for reading
Regency romance novels
In particular
As her favourite genre
Which led us on to talking about
The unusual and niche interests
And strange hobbies people have
We talked about relationships
And about modern dating
She then began telling me a story
About a date she went on
With a man she'd matched with
On a dating website
They chatted together for a while
Back and forth
About this, about that
And decided to meet up for a date
She said it was going really well
It was a good hour into the date

And they were having
An amazing time
I've found a good one here
She thought
Then, all of a sudden
A woman walked into the bar
She marched over to their table
And said
Oh, sorry for interrupting
Can I ask
Is this a date
She thought that the woman
Had forgotten some sunglasses
Or lost a wallet or something
Down the back of the sofa
That they were sitting on
The woman politely said
Oh right
Adam, can I have a word outside
With quite a panicky air about her
Like there was clearly
Something going on
She said
It was a bit like, you know
When you fall over in public
And you jump up and say

I'm fine, I'm fine
It was a bit like that
It was insane
And so
She took him outside
For a word
At that point
She was thinking to herself
This does not look good at all
After they'd been outside
The woman came back in alone
To check some details with her
She asked
Are you here with people
Did you come here on purpose
Did he invite you here
And then
Went back out to challenge him
But by that time
He'd run off into the dark
She said, for all I know
He might still be
Running around somewhere
The woman came back inside
Sat down
And they had a drink together

You had a drink with her, I asked
She replied
Yes, and then she went home
And who knows
What happened after that
It turns out
This woman
Was the man's wife
I said
So what did you and her
Talk about
During having a drink together
She said, the poor woman
Was really shaking
That she had no idea
That this was
What she was going to find
She asked
To read the text messages
That her and the man
Had sent to each other
To which she replied
Are you really sure you want to
Yes, because when I get home
He'll spin it
Into something else

So she read the messages
And luckily
They were just polite chit-chat
Before a date type messages
She said, she held onto her phone
While the woman
Read the messages
Because even then
She was still thinking
Was it some kind of
Weird crazy scam
Just to steal her cellphone
It turned out
His wife
Only checked his location
Because he was supposed to be
Attending an AA meeting
And his location
Was obviously in a bar
Because he
Was on a date with me
She said
It was not a good date after all
The barmaid
Poured her a sympathy shot
And she gave the barmaid

The man's photo
To put up behind the bar
So that if he tried it there again
With anyone else
The barmaid will be onto it
She said, what I liked to take away
From that experience
Was how the sisterhood
Came together
In that moment of crisis
As the wife
Could have been horrible to me
Or I could have been
Horrible to the wife
But we weren't
We both recognised
That we were stuck in something
That wasn't our choosing
The barmaid
Was looking out for both of us
It was nice to know
That there's people around
In a crisis
She then said
That's my most
Impressive dating story

I think
Compared to that
The foot fetishist
And the man with no teeth
Pale into insignificance
She said, he was so sweet
And that, honestly
She had always assumed
If you met somebody like that
That was up to no good
That they would be
A bit like the big bad wolf
Or like those people
That you see
In World War II films
Selling black market watches
Out of their coat
She said, he wasn't like that at all
He was really sweet
Really, my radar
For the wrong ones
Is not great
She said, at least
It was our first date
Imagine
If I was six months in

He had a daughter, she said
He had a daughter
At home in bed
God knows
What his long term plan was
Because, you know
He was telling me
That he'd been split up
For five years
But his family were at home
How was he going to
Explain that later on
She said, I assumed
This happened to everyone
On online dating
But the more I talk
To other people, she said
The more it seems
It's just me.

ABOUT THE AUTHOR

Phoenix James is an award winning Writer, Poet, Author and Spoken Word Recording Artist. He began performing his poetic words live on stages across the UK in 1998. His debut spoken word poetry album, The A.R.T.I.S.T, was released in 2000. His first limited edition printed collection of poetry, To Whom It May Concern, was published in 2003. He has toured and performed his poetry internationally since 2004. He has appeared in films, on television and radio shows, and collaborated with other artists, singer-songwriters, actors, musicians, filmmakers and producers. In 2013, he wrote, directed and produced the feature length mock documentary film, Love Freely but Pay for Sex. Phoenix James is the author of several poetry collections and has recorded and released several spoken word poetry albums including Phenzwaan Now & Forever, A Patchwork Remedy for A Broken Melody, FREE, Haven for the Tormented, With All That Said, Light Beams from the Void, and over sixty spoken word poetry singles. All are available online now and streaming everywhere worldwide.

If you enjoyed reading this book, please leave a review or comment online. The author reads every review and they help new readers discover his work.

PHOENIX JAMES

Photo by Phoenix James

Phoenix James lives in London, England.

Connect with Phoenix James on his online social media platforms via www.linktr.ee/ Phoenix_James and say you've read this book. To contact or learn more about Phoenix James and his creative journey or to receive updates via his Newsletter Mailing List, visit his official website at www.PhoenixJamesOfficial.com

CHECK OUT THE AUTHOR'S OTHER
BOOK TITLES ALSO AVAILABLE
IN PAPERBACK & EBOOK

PHOENIX JAMES
POETRY & SPOKEN WORD
COLLECTIONS:

**LOVE, SEX, ROMANCE
& OTHER BAD THINGS**

ROUTE TO DESTRUCTION

DELIRIUM OF THE WISE

**DON'T LET THE
DAFFODILS FOOL YOU**

CALL ME WHEN YOU'RE FREE

FAR FROM THE OUTSIDE

THE ONES WE DIDN'T KILL

LESSONS FROM EVERYWHERE

ANOTHER ONE FOR BURNING

A LONG BRIGHT COLD DARK SUMMER

SHAME POINT ZERO

THE SANDBAG THEORY

SOFT, SEXY & WET

BELOW BASE LEVEL

DISCOVER THESE AND MUCH MORE AT
PHOENIXJAMESOFFICIAL.COM

Phoenix James Official

www.ingramcontent.com/pod-product-compliance
Lightning Source LLC
Chambersburg PA
CBHW021227090426
42740CB00006B/414